DO YOU KNOW?

TITANIC

ALA

Scholastic Children's Books,
Euston House, 24 Eversholt Street,
London NW1 1DB, UK

A division of Scholastic Ltd
London ~ New York ~ Toronto ~ Sydney ~ Auckland
Mexico City ~ New Delhi ~ Hong Kong

Published in the UK by Scholastic Ltd, 2012

ISBN 978 1407 13142 9

Printed and bound by CPI Group (UK) Ltd, Croydon, CR0 4YY

2 4 6 8 10 9 7 5 3 1

Papers used by Scholastic Children's Books are made from woods grown in sustainable forests.

DO YOU KNOW...

- why the Titanic sank?
- how big the Titanic was?
- why they didn't spot the iceberg?
- what happened to the wreck?

No? Well keep reading and you'll soon find out...

The unsinkable Titanic

Southampton Docks, England
– 10th April, 1912

The Titanic – the Queen of the Ocean – is about to put to sea. It's the biggest ship ever built. Not just big but gigantic, awesome, a whale of a ship. It's over 260 metres long. Stand it on its end and it's almost as tall as the Eiffel Tower or the Empire State Building.

Every single link in the chain of the Titanic's anchor weighs as much as a fully grown man. On board it can carry over 3,500 passengers and crew.

This is the ship that's about to leave Southampton on her maiden voyage to New York. By midday, huge crowds have gathered on the docks to see her off. Passengers stand at the rails waving their hankies and throwing flowers into the water below. Promptly at noon, the Titanic's steam whistle blows three times and the great queen of the ocean moves on her way.

Everyone on board is excited to be on this gigantic luxury liner. They're making history. The Titanic is the biggest boat ever made and it's about to cross the Atlantic ocean on her first voyage.

Well that's what they think. Of course, they don't realize what lies in store. The Titanic is about to make history for a very different reason. In just four days time it will hit an enormous chunk of floating ice and sink like a stone.

Why did the Titanic make such a splash?

Many other boats have gone to a watery grave and been forgotten, but nobody forgets the Titanic. Though it all happened nearly a century ago people are still fascinated by the story today. The Titanic is the greatest sea disaster of all time.

So what makes it so special?

Maybe it's the old story of the bigger they come the harder they fall. The owners of the Titanic boasted that they'd made a boat so big, so strong and so powerful that it was "unsinkable". And what happened? It sank of course!

The second thing about the sinking of the Titanic is that it's such a gripping story. It's no wonder so many plays, books and films have been based on it.

Were the ship's owners tempting fate?

The Titanic was a ship of its time and the early

1900s was certainly an exciting time to be alive. There was a feeling that people were going places. And they were. One writer called it the Golden Age. The aeroplane had just been invented, the motor car was about to get into gear and life was changing at a dizzying pace. Today man has walked on the moon and satellites beam us pictures from space, but imagine the shock a hundred years ago to look up and see the first aeroplane crossing the sky.

Here are just some of the amazing inventions that were taking the world by storm:

THE TOP 4 Golden Age Firsts

1895 The first cinema is opened by the Lumière Brothers. Up to now people have only seen photographs. Now they gasp at moving pictures for the first time.

1900 **The first flight of a zeppelin – a huge cigar-shaped airship invented by Ferdinand von Zeppelin. Airships were soon overtaken by the aeroplane.**

1901 The first wireless telegraph message is transmitted across the Atlantic by Guglielmo Marconi. Messages can be sent across the world in seconds.

1903 **The Wright Brothers fly their first aeroplane.**

People in the Golden Age were anxious to get on in a hurry. But there was a downside to all the progress. In the race to find bigger, better and faster means of transport, there was always the danger that safety might take a back seat. Sooner or later a massive disaster was bound to happen.

Was anyone in the shipping industry worrying?

Nope. There was a pile of cash to be made from steamships and the owners of the Titanic – the British White Star Line – were eager to become the leading shipping company in the world. In the 1900s nobody caught a plane to America. It would have been pretty difficult because airports and passenger planes didn't exist. If you wanted to travel to the USA, you went by boat.

And when it came to building ships Britain ruled the waves. It had two big companies – Cunard and the White Star Line. Both were fighting to become the world's number one shipping line. At first it was Cunard who led the way by breaking the speed record for getting to America. The Cunard liners – the Lusitania and Mauritania – could cross the North Atlantic in under five days. The White Star Line fought back. If they couldn't beat Cunard for speed they'd find other ways to sell tickets. Why not build the biggest ship ever? Not only was Titanic the biggest, it was also the last word in elegance and luxury.

How BIG are we talking?

OK, let's get down to details. Imagine you are about to step on board the biggest ship ever built. What do you see?

Your first impression is the sheer mind-boggling size of the Titanic. From end to end it's a sixth of a mile long – that's about three times the length of a football pitch. The rudder alone is as big as a house and the ship needs three anchors to hold it in port. The Titanic boasts eight decks which means it would take you most of the morning just to explore it.

Titanic wasn't just the biggest ship afloat, it was the largest moving object ever made by man.

Yet the Titanic's size is only part of the picture,

the ship is also about power and luxury. It has three huge engines – the most powerful ever built – and four funnels (though one is actually a fake – don't tell anyone!).

As you wander the passenger decks you'll find no expense has been spared to make you comfortable. There's a swimming pool, a top-class restaurant and a gym equipped with the latest exercise machines. Every detail has been thought of. In the bathrooms in first-class there is even a special holder to park your fat cigar!

So how safe is it supposed to be?

Well, everyone just assumes the ship is safe. A boat that big has to be safe – er... doesn't it?

Ⓐ Cargo
Ⓑ 2nd class staterooms
Ⓒ 1st class smokeroom
Ⓓ A la carte restaurant
Ⓔ Aft 1st class staircase

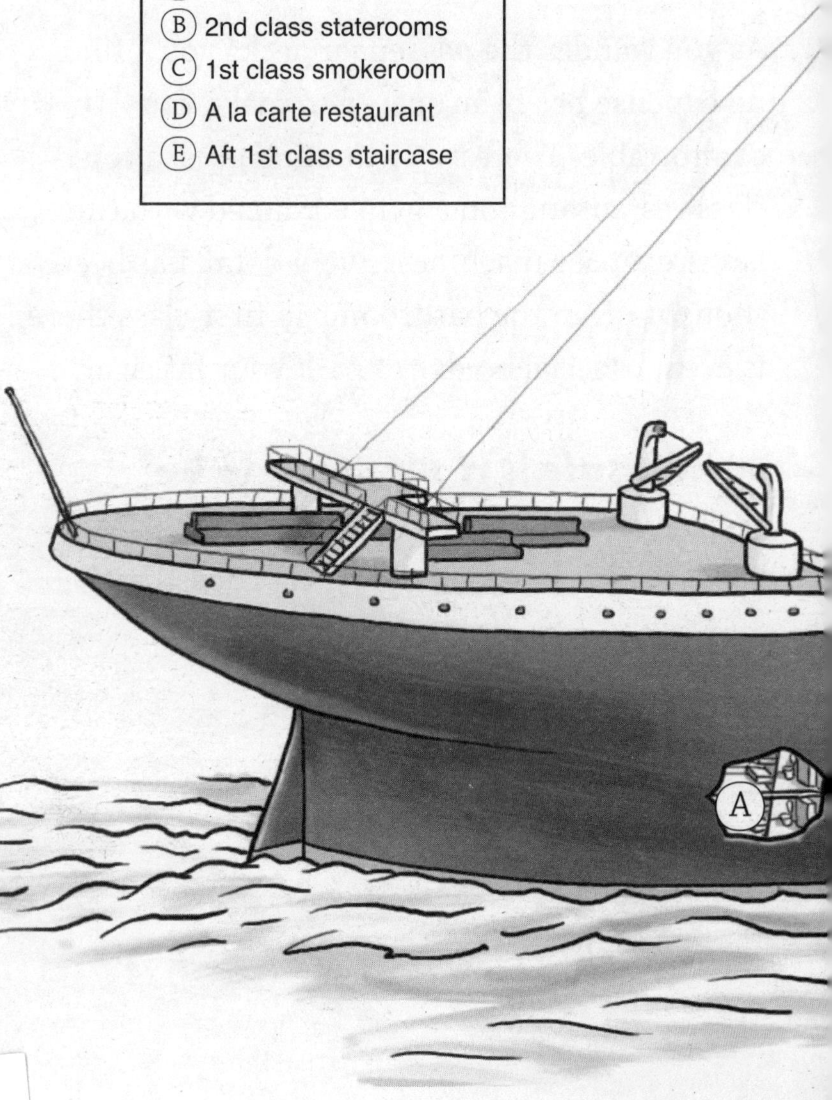

C
E
D
B

F
G
H
I
O
P

- (F) 1st class staterooms
- (G) Gymnasium
- (H) Marconi room
- (I) Forward grand staircase
- (J) Crows nest
- (K) Crew quarters
- (L) Third class births
- (M) Cargo
- (N) Swimming bath
- (O) Turkish bath
- (P) 3rd class dining room
- (Q) Officers quarters
- (R) Bridge

Are you sailing comfortably?

Welcome aboard, shipmates. So you've waved goodbye, the ship has steamed out of Southampton and you are on your way to America. Time to have a proper look around.

First things first, who's on board?

The short answer is: almost everyone who is anyone in 1912. The Titanic is swarming with millionaires and celebrities. Being a famous ship, everyone wants to get on board for its maiden (first) voyage. After all, if you're rich, what better way of showing off than buying a first class ticket on the world's most expensive steamship?

In the Golden Age of the 1900s it's easy to tell the rich and poor apart. The rich are stinking rich and the poor are just stinking. Passengers on the Titanic are divided into first, second and third class. Those with pots of money naturally travel first class and enjoy every luxury. Third class passengers meanwhile travel in steerage (so called because it's at the back, near the rudder which does the steering).

First class passengers can choose from three electric lifts to ride between decks. Second class have only one, while in third class you take the stairs!

DO YOU KNOW?

There's one other excellent reason for travelling first class – you have a much better chance of surviving if the ship goes down, simply because you're at the top of the boat nearest the lifeboats.

Who can I bump into in First Class?

So you're clutching your first class ticket and ready to mingle with some celebs. Let's take a stroll along the promenade deck and see who's in the first class smoking room. Here are just a few of the rich and famous you can rub shoulders with…

Colonel John Jacob Astor

Property tycoon who owns more hotels and skyscrapers than any man in New York. Worth a cool $100 million, Astor is the richest man on board, though that hasn't made him flavour of the month in New York's high society. Astor caused a scandal by divorcing his wife and marrying a younger woman, 18-year-old Madeleine Force. Astor and his young wife have been abroad for a long holiday while things cool down back home. Now, with Madeleine pregnant, they're heading home to New York.

Benjamin Guggenheim

Swiss American who made his pile in mining. Benjamin will typify the "stiff upper lip" attitude of many first class passengers during the disaster.

Isidor and Ida Straus

A sweet elderly couple from New York. They run Macy's department store, which is a bit like owning Harrods in London.

Sir Cosmo and Lady Lucile Duff Gordon

Fashionable, pottily-named English aristocrats. Sir Cosmo is a baronet who has fenced for England in the Olympics. His wife, Lady Lucile, is a top dress designer with a chain of shops in London, Paris and New York. Lucile is credited with the startling idea of models actually moving around while modelling dresses, instead of acting like stuffed dummies.

Where are all the riff-raff?

On another deck. (You don't expect them to be allowed into first class do you?)

Passengers in second class are more likely to be English professional classes visiting friends or family in America. As for third class passengers, most of them are emigrants – heading to America to make their fortunes. In their dreams anyway. In third class you can meet butchers, bricklayers, clerks and servants. They've heard America is the land of opportunity. In steerage there's almost every nationality from French to Polish, and Russian to Chinese. Whether America would have lived up to their dreams most people never found out. Less than half of those in third class would ever set eyes on New York.

Who's the chap with the whiskers?

The Captain of the Titanic, 59-year-old Edward Smith. Smith is an old sea salt and a popular figure known as the "Millionaire's Captain". He has sailed on Titanic's sister ship, the Olympic, and is now trusted with the safe-keeping of the jewel in the White Star's crown. It will be Smith's last great voyage before retirement – but sadly he won't live to hang up his peaked cap.

WHAT THEY SAID

"I have never been in any accident of any sort worth speaking about... I never saw a wreck and have never been wrecked."

CAPTAIN EDWARD SMITH

Another high-ranking crew member is Second Officer Charles Lightoller. He'll be in charge of loading the lifeboats, so you might want to stay close to him.

Is that everyone?

No. There's one more VIP (very important person) on board. He's called J Bruce Ismay. Ismay hasn't got a ticket – not because he's a stowaway but because he's the Director of the White Star Line. The boss. He probably thought it would make good publicity to sail on the maiden voyage of his own ship. As it turned out, stepping on board the Titanic was the worst decision he ever made.

Should I be worried?

Don't be ridiculous! No one on board imagines for a moment that the great ship could actually go down. Remember, according to the makers the Titanic is unsinkable. And besides, there are plenty of delights on board to stop you getting gloomy. Why not take a wander back through first class and see what you can find?

You might like to hop on an exercise bike in the gym or brush up on your squash with the squash pro. You could get steamed up in the Turkish bath or cool down in the luxury swimming pool. Afterwards, you could enjoy a cup of coffee in the fashionable Café Parisien or just sit back and relax, listening to the jolly tunes of the Titanic's resident band. The ship has even got its own barber's shop in case you need a quick trim. For first class passengers the Titanic is a floating palace of pleasure.

Anyone for a game of cards?

Card games such as bridge or poker are a favourite in first class. But keep a sharp eye out for professional gamblers, such as Harry "Kid" Homer. Tricksters like Homer haven't come on the trip for a holiday. They're planning to take some money off some of the rich passengers on board. Even when the boat starts to sink a card game will still be going on. OK, the players might feel the iceberg scrape the ship and even notice the decks begin to tilt but no way are they going to abandon their game!

What can I do in steerage?

In the cheap seats in third class, people are making their own entertainment. They play ball games on deck or just talk about what they'll do in America when they get there. Some have brought their own instruments and occasionally a pipe or fiddle strikes up a tune and gets people dancing.

WHAT THEY SAID

"Everything has been done in regard to the furniture and fittings to make the first class accommodation more than equal to that provided in the finest hotels on shore."

THE SHIPBUILDER'S JOURNAL

"I enjoyed myself as if I were in a summer palace on the seashore, surrounded with every comfort."

TITANIC PASSENGER

So when did it all go wrong?

For many in first class the first four days at sea are an endless round of dinner parties, cards, dancing and swapping stories in the comfortable smoking room. "The days passed too quickly, I felt as if I would like them to go on until the end of time," said first class passenger, Mrs Rene Harris.

On that fateful Sunday night, Captain Smith is the guest of honour at a dinner party hosted by George Widener (the Wideners are Philadelphia's richest family). With the ship reaching the last leg of its journey everyone is looking forward to reaching New York. Passengers are making bets on the probable time of the run across the Atlantic.

Owner J Bruce Ismay boasts that the Titanic will certainly set a faster time than its sister ship, the Olympic. After dinner, Captain Smith lights up a cigar and listens to the orchestra entertaining passengers with light music. He's feeling relaxed and at ease. Meanwhile, down in the second class dining room a church service is taking place. (It is Sunday after all.) The Reverend Ernest Carter has invited passengers to sing hymns with him. About 100 passengers attend and the hymns are chosen by passengers calling out their favourites. Second class passenger Lawrence Beesley said afterwards: "It was curious to see how many chose hymns dealing with dangers at sea. I noticed the hushed tone with which all sang the hymn 'For those in peril on the sea'."

The singing finishes at about 10 o'clock in the evening. Less than two hours later the Titanic will strike disaster.

That sinking feeling

The Titanic hit a large chunk of ice and sank. Those are the cold facts.

But why didn't the crew see a thumping great iceberg in their path? Why weren't they prepared?

OK, here's how it happened...

The North Atlantic Ocean – 14th April 9pm

It's Sunday evening. The sea is flat calm and the weather is cold. It's a brilliant moonless, starry night as Captain Smith says good night to his dinner companions. He calls in at the bridge to chat for a while to Second Officer Lightoller. They have no reason to be more alert than usual. What's there to worry about? The voyage is almost over. Everything's gone smoothly. True, the radio room has picked up ice warnings from other ships, but why pay attention to them when you're in an unsinkable ship?

FIRST WARNING: 9 am

Another ship, the Caronia, warns of ice up ahead. Captain Smith passes on the information to his officers.

SECOND WARNING: 11.40 am

A second ship reports icebergs in the area. This time the captain passes the message on to J Bruce Ismay before lunch. The White Star director puts the warning in his pocket and casually shows it to a few passengers over lunch.

"I suppose you are going to slow her down?" asks one passenger.

"Oh no," replies Ismay. "On the contrary we are going to let her run a great deal faster and get out of it."

THIRD WARNING: 7.30 pm

The Californian warns of "three large icebergs"

50 miles ahead of the Titanic. Captain Smith never gets the message as none of the crew like to interrupt his dinner.

FOURTH WARNING: 9.40 pm

Another liner, the Mesaba, reports “a great number of large icebergs” in the area where the Titanic is cruising. The wireless operator on duty, Jack Phillips, sticks the message under a paperweight and forgets all about it. He’s far too busy with the mountain of telegrams he has to send to New York for passengers on board.

By now Captain Smith, believing that all's well, has gone to his cabin. He's left instructions with Lightoller to wake him if the weather got hazy. But Lightoller doesn't need to wake him – the iceberg does that!

Where did the iceberg come from?

You've probably seen pictures of icebergs, large floating chunks of ice which have broken off from a glacier. "Berg" is a Scandinavian word which means "mountain". And some of these icebergs were like floating mountains. The iceberg drifting towards the Titanic is only a middleweight at about 500,000 tons. Nevertheless, it's over ten times as heavy as the Titanic. The crash about to happen is rather like a bicycle running into the side of an elephant.

10 PM – FULL SPEED AHEAD

The ship continues cruising at a brisk speed of 22.5 knots – the fastest it has gone all journey. As the Titanic speeds on through the night, the

passengers tap their feet to the band or sleep peacefully in their cabins. Up on the bridge, Officer Lightoller is replaced for his watch by First Officer Murdoch.

11.39 PM — ICEBERG AHEAD!

Tonight the Titanic has two lookouts on duty – Reginald Lee and Fred Fleet. They are watching from the crow's nest high up on the mast.

Fred Fleet is the first to spot the whopping iceberg, lying dead in their path. "There's ice ahead," he says to Lee.

Sounding the alarm, he rings the bell three times and telephones the bridge. Sixth Officer James Moody answers the call. "Iceberg right ahead!" warns Fleet urgently.

"Thank you," answers Moody politely, as if he's just been told that tea is served. The monster berg is now less than 500 metres away. In thirty seconds disaster will strike.

First Officer Murdoch, however, is doing his best to avoid a crash. "Hard a port!" he orders. (The man at the wheel knows that means turn left.) Murdoch signals the engine room to cut the power and go into reverse. His actions save the Titanic from crashing head-first into the iceberg. But unfortunately that only makes things worse.

The ship would probably have survived a head-on crash. Instead it passed the iceberg on its left side.

And then it happens...

11.40 PM – THE CRUNCH

The iceberg scrapes along the side of the Titanic with a sickening sound of ripping metal. A few chunks of ice even break off and land on deck.

But the real damage is happening out of sight, under the water. The iceberg tears through the hull of the ship and water immediately starts to pour in below decks. The Titanic is in big trouble.

Does everyone panic?

That's the funny part – they don't. In fact some of the passengers even sleep right through the crash! The scrape with the iceberg lasts about ten seconds. But not everyone hears the moment of disaster. Even those who do fail to grasp the full danger of the situation.

WHAT THEY SAID

"It did not seem to me there was any great impact at all. It was as though we went over about a thousand marbles."

MRS J STUART WHITE, PASSENGER

"If I had had a brimful glass of water in my hand, not a drop would have been spilled."

JACK THAYER, PASSENGER

"It was as though someone had drawn a giant finger all along the side of the boat."

LADY LUCILLE DUFF GORDON, PASSENGER

So what's the damage?

The ship will sink slowly at first – and it will be two and a half hours before she plunges to the bottom of the sea. Maybe this is why few passengers realize they're in danger until it's too late.

Captain Smith soon knows it's serious. Hearing the scrape, he takes the ship's designer, Thomas Andrews, below to investigate the damage. The Titanic is fitted with the latest watertight compartments below decks. These could be sealed with electric doors so that even if two compartments are flooded the ship can still float. But what Smith and Andrews see confirms their worst fears. In a mere ten minutes, 4.25 metres of water has flooded into five of the ship's compartments. At that moment they realize that the Titanic will sink as sure as a sack of spuds. Captain Smith goes to the wireless room and orders a signal for help. Unless a nearby boat can help them, time is running out.

Does anyone get the message?

The good news is there is a ship in the area. In fact, the steamship Californian is so close to the Titanic that they can actually see each other. The bad news is that the Californian's wireless operator has gone off duty. He's snoring in bed with the radio turned off, deaf to Titanic's cries for help.

Luckily, one officer on the Californian does see the distress rockets from the Titanic. After five rockets Herbert Stone suspects something must be wrong. He goes to tell his captain who is dozing in the map room.

So the Captain turns his boat round and steams to the rescue like a hero?

Actually um... no. Captain Stanley Lord has more important matters on his mind like getting a good kip.

Afterwards Lord claims he was too sleepy to take in the message he was given. He even tried to claim that the boat they'd seen wasn't the Titanic at all!

Finally, it seems to Herbert Stone that the mystery ship is moving away. Herbert is wrong. The Titanic isn't moving off, it's sinking below the ocean.

Don't panic! (It's all under control)

WHAT THEY SAID

"There was no indication of panic or hysteria; no cries of fear, and no running to and fro to discover what was the matter, why we had been summoned on deck with lifebelts and what was to be done with us now we were there."

LAWRENCE BEESLEY, PASSENGER

12PM – WE FORGOT TO MENTION...

Shortly after midnight Captain Smith orders the lifeboats to be made ready. He does so, knowing one terrible fact. He doesn't mention this fact to anyone. The truth is, the lifeboats hold a maximum of 1,178 people. Yet on the Titanic that night are 2,228 passengers and crew. It doesn't take a genius to tell you that doesn't add up. Only about half the Titanic's passengers can be crammed into the lifeboats. That means not everyone will be saved.

How did the White Star Line come to make such a bone-headed blunder?

Originally the plans for the Titanic called for 64 wooden lifeboats. But plans change. With the addition of the watertight compartments, lifeboats were no longer a top priority.

DO YOU KNOW?

The Titanic had only sixteen lifeboats for over 2,000 people.

Even this number was more than safety standards required in 1912. Obviously, no one stopped to think what would happen if a boat started to sink with everyone on board!

12.15 AM – FUR COATS AND PYJAMAS

Passengers begin to file up on deck in whatever they are wearing. Some have their lifebelts fastened over fur coats and dinner jackets, others are in their dressing gowns and pyjamas. There isn't time to rescue their luggage. Teacher Lawrence Beesley puts on his warm jacket and tucks two of his favourite books into his pockets. Steward James Johnson is more practical, stuffing four oranges into his shirt in case he gets hungry.

Nobody is panicking or screaming, probably because no one believes that the ship is actually sinking. After all, the ship's lights are still on, the stewards are laying the tables for breakfast and the band is still playing cheerful ditties in the dining room. What's there to worry about?

12.45 AM – FORM A QUEUE

It's one hour after the iceberg struck, and the first lifeboat is finally loaded. The rule on the

Titanic is "women and children first". And most passengers stick to this as the most civilized way to behave. A few men do try to barge their way into a lifeboat, but officers armed with guns soon persuade them to take a step back. One report tells of an officer actually shooting a man who tried to force his way into a boat. On the other hand the women aren't exactly fighting to get into the lifeboats. To them, they look small and fragile. Even worse, the drop down to the sea looks an awful long way. Who wants to sit in a lifeboat being lowered down on flimsy ropes? Much better to stay on the ship – it seems so big and safe.

When a steward pleads with three women strolling the deck to get into a lifeboat they reply, "We're all right, Steward, the ship can't sink." In their minds, anyone getting into a lifeboat would only have to go to the tiresome bother of rowing back to the ship when the alarm was over. How wrong could they be? Eventually some women are picked up by the crew and practically thrown into the lifeboats.

Despite the shortage of lifeboats, more lives could have been saved. Around 700 people make it into the lifeboats, but that still leaves room for another 475. The first lifeboat is lowered with only 28 people on board – leaving 37 empty seats!

So are the crew blind or barmy?

For starters, Titanic's crew has never been through a proper lifeboat drill. They aren't sure whether the lifeboats can be safely lowered over the side fully loaded. (In fact they can.)

Secondly, neither the officers or the passengers realize the urgency of getting people into lifeboats. It's only when the distress rockets start to be fired that people start to believe the ship might actually be sinking. Then the first signs of panic show. As lifeboat number 5 is lowered, four men make a desperate bid to escape and jump into it.

DO YOU KNOW?

One man, weighing a beefy 250 pounds, finds something to break his fall. Unfortunately it's a woman passenger who he knocks out cold!

1.15 AM – TIME RUNNING OUT

By this time around 1,500 people are left on the ship. For them the prospects look bleak. The front part of the boat (the bow) is sinking ever deeper into the water. They can feel the deck tip beneath their feet.

Some desperate passengers try to rush lifeboat number 14. It's already overloaded and Fifth Officer Lowe fires his revolver three times over the side of the ship to warn them off. A frightened young boy who has managed to jump into the boat is dragged out by Lowe at the point of his gun.

As the water creeps up inch by inch, some of the crew are still offering normal service. Crazily, the gym instructor is helping passengers on the exercise equipment as the boat continues to sink. On deck, the ship's orchestra goes on playing waltzes and ragtime melodies to calm the passengers.

2.05 AM – THE LAST LIFEBOAT

The last wooden lifeboat is launched just before two o'clock. John Jacob Astor, the millionaire, watches his pregnant wife get into the boat and waves her off as it descends. (Astor will go down wearing his gold watch, gold and diamond cufflinks and diamond ring. His pockets are stuffed with notes to the tune of $2,440.)

Among the passengers on the last lifeboat are two little French boys, Michel and Edmond, who are passed to the crew by their father.

Five minutes later the bow of the ship gives a lurch and plunges deeper into the water. There's a sudden rush of passengers towards the back of the boat and many jump or fall from the ship.

2.17 AM – SWAN SONG

As the deck rises higher and higher, the orchestra plays on. The water closes in, and bandleader Wallace Hartley finally gives his musicians permission to go. Nobody moves. As the Titanic goes down, the orchestra are playing their last song. Some say it was the hymn "Nearer my God to Thee".

At last the stern tips so far it's right out of the water. People scramble for safety or jump overboard as everything goes sliding down the deck. The ship's lights flicker, then go out. Then, with a sickening sound, the Titanic breaks in half between the two funnels and the bow plunges underwater. It's the great ship's last death rattle. Finally it sinks beneath the waves, creating a great whirlpool that sucks everything into its wake.

What about the captain?

Some people say the last thing Captain Smith shouted before the ship went down was "Be British!" Was he kidding? Half the passengers on board were American, French, Russian or Chinese! Smith probably meant that people should keep a British stiff upper lip and face death honourably. Some passengers took his advice, others just tried to save their necks.

Who sank with style?

Ben Guggenheim spent his last hours changing into evening dress so that he could go down like a gentleman. He told a steward that he doubted that the men would get off the boat. "I am willing to remain and play the man's game if there are not enough boats for more than the women and children," he declared. "I won't die here like a beast. Tell my wife... I played the game out straight and to the end."

American artist Frank Millet and Major Archibald Butt, also kept their dignity to the end. They retired to the first-class smoking room and calmly dealt a last hand of cards.

Maybe the most touching story of the Titanic belongs to Isidor and Ida Straus – the owners of Macy's famous store in New York. The elderly couple should have been in lifeboat number 8 but, despite his age, Mr Straus refused any special treatment. He wouldn't get in until all the women and children were safely off the ship. His wife Ida was not to be outdone in stubbornness. She wouldn't be parted from her husband's side, saying, "We have been living together for many years and where you go, I go."

Ida's last act was to give her fur coat to her maid to ward off the cold. The Strauses were last seen sitting together on a deck bench, calmly watching the lifeboats fill as the boat sank lower and lower. They must have known their chances of survival in the freezing water were zero.

So were they all heroes?

Not all. Remember Sir Cosmo Duff Gordon and his fashionable wife, Lady Lucile? They made it into a half-full lifeboat and saved their own skins. As the ship went down they could hear the desperate cries of survivors in the water but they refused to go back. They were afraid that their lifeboat might be swamped by people trying to get on board. Sir Cosmo may have had a knighthood but he was no gentleman. Some say he paid the crew not to turn around and go back for survivors. Cosmo's explanation was that he gave them money to make up for their lost possessions. A likely story!

Was it only the toffs who misbehaved?

Not at all. Maybe the strangest Titanic tale, surrounds little Frank Aks, a baby who survived the shipwreck. Little Filly – as he was called – was snatched from his mum's arms and actually thrown into a lifeboat. Lucky for him a woman called Elizabeth Nye was on hand to catch him.

Meanwhile, in the confusion, Filly's mum Leah was prevented from getting into the same boat as her baby.

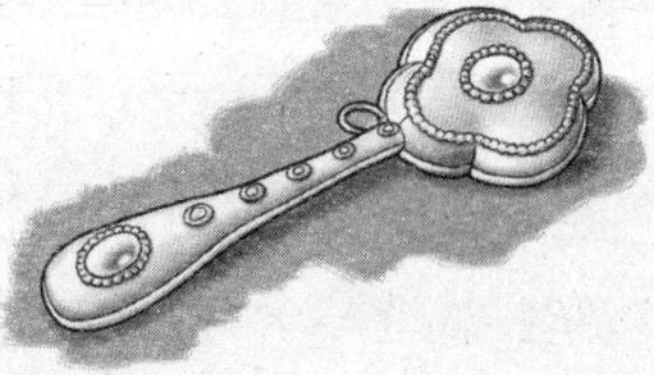

Eventually the survivors were rescued by a ship called the Carpathia. Imagine Leah's relief when she saw her little Filly safe and sound. But Elizabeth Nye had taken a liking to the bouncing babe. When Leah asked for her son back, Nye claimed the baby was hers! The captain of the Carpathia had to be called in to settle the furious quarrel between the two women. Luckily he was quickly able to guess which woman was the baby's true mother. How did he know? Leah knew her baby had a strawberry birthmark on his chest and Nye had to admit she was telling a lie.

WHAT THEY SAID

"I watched groups of the almost fifteen hundred people still aboard, clinging in clusters or bunches, like swarming bees, only to fall in masses, pairs or singly, as the great after-part of the ship, 200 feet of it, rose into the sky."

JACK THAYER, PASSENGER

"The cries of the drowning, floating across the quiet sea, filled us with stupefaction. We longed to return and rescue at least some of the drowning, but we knew it was impossible. The boat was filled to standing room, and to return would mean the swamping of us all, and so the captain-stoker told his crew to row away from the cries."

LAWRENCE BEESLEY, PASSENGER

"Fortunately, the scene that followed was shrouded in darkness. Less fortunately, the calm, still silence carried every sound with startling distinctness."

SECOND OFFICER LIGHTOLLER

A big Stink

The Titanic was the biggest disaster story of the century. For weeks it hogged the front pages of the papers in both Britain and America. As soon as news broke, people started to ask awkward questions. Why did the ship sink? What went wrong? Who was to blame? There was a nasty smell hanging over the whole disaster. Some people wanted to hush up the true story, but the outcry was too great. A public inquiry was called and uncomfortable facts soon started to come to light.

Weren't the papers quick to sniff out the story?

Oddly enough the Titanic story was slow to break. To start with there were lots of wild rumours and false reports going round. Anxious relatives waiting for news were hopeful one minute and crushed the next. Crowds gathered outside the White Star offices in New York and England.

The New York Times ran the first story on the morning of the disaster.

TITANIC STRIKES ICEBERG!

The newspaper had picked up a message at 1.20 am saying that the Titanic was sinking and had called for help.

They didn't know any other details.

Later that morning a second story completely contradicted the New York Times' version.

TITANIC SAFE AND ON ITS WAY TO HALIFAX!

Halifax? So how did it turn up in the middle of Yorkshire?

Well, actually they meant Halifax in Nova Scotia. But the story was a result of a mix-up with a wireless message about an oil tanker which was being towed into port. Information was hard to come by and people (especially the Titanic's owners) were eager to believe good news.

Finally, the true story got through 14 hours after the Titanic had sunk. It was picked up at 4.35 in the afternoon by David Sarnoff, a 21-year-old wireless operator at Wanamaker's department store in New York. The news was worse than anyone could have feared.

TITANIC SUNK – 1,500 DROWNED!

Bet someone cashed in on the story?

The Titanic story was so hot it was worth a lot of money. One person who realized that was Harold Bride – the Titanic wireless operator who survived. Bride didn't reply to messages from the navy or the press asking for news of the doomed ship, probably because he was under orders from his employers – the Marconi Wireless Company. Harold got a message saying: "Keep your mouth shut and hold your story. It is fixed for you so you will get big money." Marconi had struck a deal with the New York Times. Bride was paid $1,000 for his exclusive story (a small fortune in those days). At the inquiry, both Marconi and Harold Bride denied that they hushed up the story to make sure they got their exclusive.

Surely journalists weren't as sneaky then as they are today?

Don't you believe it! Reporters were in a frenzy to get the inside story on the Titanic. When the Carpathia docked in New York with the wreck's survivors, no reporters were allowed on board. One reporter tried to force his way up the gang-plank and got a punch in the jaw for his pains. Another reporter tried to trick his way on board. He pretended to be ill by filling his mouth with foam. Then he demanded to see his sister who he claimed was one of the passengers! When this barmy trick didn't work he tried to bribe his way on board, offering $200.

DO YOU KNOW

When the true story of the disaster finally spilled out, the White Star offices in New York were under siege from people desperate for news of their loved ones. Police had to be called in to control the crowd.

No doubt they wanted a few questions answered?

Obviously, the public wanted to know why the disaster had happened. In America a US Senate (government) inquiry began only five days after the disaster.

In Britain, the Board of Trade held their own inquiry starting on 2nd May. But few people had much faith in the outcome. For one thing, whoever had passed the Titanic as safe to go to sea had a lot of questions to answer. And who was that? Yes – right first time. It was the British Board of Trade! They were hardly likely to find themselves guilty were they?

So who got the blame?

The American press needed a bad guy to pin the blame on. There was one obvious candidate who represented the White Star Line and was on board at the time of the disaster. The papers pointed the finger at the Titanic's owner, J Bruce Ismay. The press took to calling him "J Brute Ismay". They even said that the White Star's emblem should be changed from a white star to a white liver (for cowards). Perhaps Ismay's real crime was that he survived the wreck, while over a thousand passengers on his ship died.

Hang on a minute! Ismay got out alive?

Ismay's own version of how he escaped never made much sense. He claimed that there were no other passengers around when he stepped into the last lifeboat to be lowered. Others reckoned that he made the boat by shoving women and children out of the way. One rumour going round said he ordered a lifeboat for himself, manned by a handpicked crew. Ismay may not have been as cold-hearted as that, but how he really escaped will always remain a mystery.

What's certain is that he didn't do anything to

improve his popularity after the shipwreck. When the survivors were picked up, Ismay didn't lift a finger to see that they were looked after. Instead, he hid himself away and avoided talking to anyone. He was busy making arrangements to scurry back to England when the American inquiry forced him to stay as a witness.

What was his defence, then?

It could be summed up in three words: "I knew nothing." He claimed he didn't know anything about the Titanic's design. He didn't know what speed it should have been going at. He couldn't even say whether his cabin was on the port (left) or starboard (right) side of the ship. (He probably needed to look in his hat to remember his own name!) Some critics claimed it was Ismay who made Captain Smith go faster than he should have done. But Smith was drowned, so the truth will never be known. Somebody had to be the villain of the piece and Ismay got the job. Probably his biggest mistake was that he refused to take any responsibility for what happened. Quite possibly his nerves never recovered from the shock of the shipwreck.

> **WHAT THEY SAID**
>
> *"I may say that at the time Mr Ismay did not seem to me to be in a mental state to decide anything... He was obsessed with the idea, and kept repeating that he ought to have gone down with the ship because he found that some women had gone down."*
>
> SECOND OFFICER HERBERT LIGHTOLLER

So Ismay wasn't punished? Not even a little bit?

Neither the American nor the British inquiry found anything to pin on Ismay. The person they did blame was poor old Captain Stanley Lord. Remember Lord, the captain of the

Californian, the ship that didn't race to the rescue? Lord's officers saw the distress rockets go up and reported them but their captain did nothing.

At the inquiry Lord's defence was as feeble as Ismay's. He said he didn't realize the rockets were distress signals and was half asleep when he was told about them. Lord always claimed that the Californian was too far away to have helped the Titanic in any case. His supporters claim there was a third ship in the area at the time but no one's ever identified this mystery ship. In any case, it seems harsh to blame Lord when so many other people got off lightly.

Who gave evidence?

The star witness of both investigations was Second Officer Lightoller. Not only was he the senior surviving officer but he was also a convincing speaker. In a nutshell Lightoller's view was that nobody was to blame. He said the

Titanic was just plain unlucky to run into a big blue iceberg which was hard to spot on a dark night.

He would say that, wouldn't he?

Lightoller didn't want to blame his employers and risk losing his job. The authorities were happy to go along with his cosy version of events. No one was to blame – that let the Board of Trade off the hook for letting the Titanic go to sea. All in all, the British inquiry was one big cover-up. It's true the disaster couldn't be blamed on one person, but still, mistakes were made. Titanic mistakes.

WHAT THEY SAID

"What do you think I am? Do you believe I'm the sort that would have left the ship as long as there were any women and children aboard her? That's the thing that hurts... because it's so false and baseless."

J BRUCE ISMAY, WHITE STAR DIRECTOR

"It is, in my opinion, impossible to fix Captain Smith with blame."
LORD MERSEY, HEAD OF THE BRITISH INQUIRY

"The Board of Trade had passed that ship as in all respects fit for the sea... Now the Board of Trade was holding an inquiry into the loss of that ship. Hence the whitewash brush."
OFFICER CHARLES LIGHTOLLER

THE TOP 4 Things that went wrong

4. Safety laws were hopeless
Board of Trade rules said that big ships had to have at least 16 lifeboats. The Titanic met safety regulations, but the rules were as useless as a paper umbrella. Only half the passengers on board could

get into the lifeboats. What's more, third class passengers had no chance of reaching the boat deck until it was too late.

3. The lifeboats were half empty The passengers and crew didn't get the message that the ship was actually going down. As a result, the lifeboats were lowered with 400 empty seats. Many more lives should have been saved.

2. The ship was going way too fast
The Titanic had plenty of warning that there was ice around, but it continued to cruise at high speed. No one believed that icebergs were a real danger.

1. The design was faulty. The Titanic boasted a double-plated extra-thick

bottom. Unfortunately, the iceberg ripped into the ship's side which was not doubly reinforced. Added to that, the "extra safe" watertight compartments flooded and proved useless.

When the Titanic set sail from Southampton on 10th April, 1912 no one dreamed that it could sink. The trouble was the big shipping companies were obsessed with speed, power and luxury. They completely forgot about the one thing that really mattered. Safety.

So it was human error that caused the Titanic to sink?

Maybe there's a more spooky explanation. Many people told of weird experiences connected with the disaster.
One newspaper reported that as many as 6,000 people had made plans to board the Titanic but for some reason didn't.

DO YOU KNOW?

In fact the ship had capacity for 3,500 but it was only two-thirds full when it left England.

Many of the people who planned to travel on the ill-fated ship claimed they had a feeling that something bad was going to happen. Take businessman Mr Middleton, who was going to sail to America on the Titanic. He had two dreams in which he saw the ship sinking. What would you have done? Middleton changed his plans and lived to tell the tale.

Since that April night in 1912, many other ghostly stories about the Titanic have surfaced.

Ghost stories? Let's hear them!

One day, Captain Peter Pryall ran into an old seamate of his, Captain Edward Smith. Rather nervously, Pryall approached him. "Captain

Smith, how are you?" he asked.

Smith turned a pale, bearded face to him, and replied that he was quite well, but he was sorry he couldn't stop to chat. Pryall followed his friend to a railway station and saw him buy a ticket to Washington. Smith's parting words were: "Be good shipmate, until we meet again." Pryall watched the figure of the captain depart and felt a cold chill pass over him. Three months before, Smith had drowned on the Titanic!

Spooky! Did anyone else come back from the dead?

Doris Williams had always been scared of ships and the sea. In 1960 she consulted a minister called Reverend Young about the problem. Under hypnosis, Doris revealed that in a previous life she had been a man named Blackwell who went down on the Titanic. Doris even knew his address. Later investigation showed that there really was a passenger called Stephen Blackwell who had drowned.

But could anything sinister have made the ship go down?

Another Titanic passenger was W.T. Stead – one of Britain's most brilliant journalists. Stead had a keen interest in spiritualism and believed the dead could be contacted. He was warned by several fortune tellers not to board the Titanic but he ignored their advice. He firmly believed that he'd meet his end at the hands of a mob, so why should he worry about a sea journey? While on the board the Titanic, Stead told a story about an Egyptian mummy with a mysterious inscription on the case. Anyone who uttered the words of this message, he said, would come to a sticky end. Stead himself wasn't bothered by such superstitions and he spoke the fateful words. Just two days later he drowned – and took the Titanic with him!

Titanic – the never-ending story

So that was that? End of story?

Not quite. The Titanic continued to make waves long after the ship went down.

THE TOP 4 Things to Change

4. New shipping laws required more lifeboats
3. Stronger pumps
2. More wireless officers so they can work in shifts
1. International ice patrol

The mania for building bigger and bigger ships also faded away. Yet the one thing that refused to go away was the story of the Titanic itself. People continued to talk and write about it. For one thing, the shipwreck was still at the bottom of the Atlantic Ocean and the answers to many mysteries lay down there in the deep.

Why not raise the wreck?

Only five days after the tragedy, the son of millionaire John Jacob Astor announced he was going to raise the hull of the ship to find his father's body. His plan was abandoned when Astor's body was recovered from the sea. Nevertheless, others kept alive the dream of raising the Titanic. The ship had quickly become a legend, surrounded by rumours of fabulous gold and precious jewels.

Any truth in the rumours?

They were complete rubbish, but since when did truth get in the way of a good story?

Did anyone get to find out?

There were many schemes to raise the ship – some clever, and many crackpot. In 1913, an architect named Charles Smith came up with a plan. His idea was to send down a submarine and attach electro-magnets to the ship, which would then pull it to the surface. He worked out that the project would take 162 men and a budget of $1.5 million. Funnily enough, at that point everyone lost interest in the idea. Other schemes surfaced, but got nowhere. Then came two world wars and the idea of raising the Titanic was forgotten for around 40 years.

Why did it make a comeback?

In 1955 Walter Lord published his book about the Titanic disaster – A Night To Remember. A film followed three years later, and Titanic mania was back with a vengeance. More wild schemes to raise the wreck followed in the 1960s. One English treasure hunter was Douglas Woolley – a worker in a sock factory. (Where else, with a name like that?) Woolley also claimed to be the legal owner of the Titanic. His dodgy claim was based on his ownership of a share in the White Star Line. Since White Star were the original owners and Woolley had the last share in the company, he reckoned that made him the owner of the Titanic.

So Woolley was keen to raise the wreck of "his" boat?

His idea was to fill the sunken ship with nylon balloons. The balloons could then be inflated and they'd float the wreck to the surface, leaving Woolley to grab any goodies left on board. Sadly, being a humble sock worker, he didn't have the cash to back his scheme.

Woolley's inflated ideas sound quite sensible compared to some of the potty schemes of the 1970s. One idea was to fill the ship with thousands of bags of Vaseline jelly. Once the jelly hardened, it would float the wreck upwards. Or what about ping-pong balls, said another bright spark? Pump the ship with millions of ping-pong balls, and it would just pop up like a... well, like a bag of ping pong balls!

And who wins the prize for the pottiest plan?

It has to be operation iceberg. This scheme

involved wrapping the wreck in wire mesh and then spraying it with liquid nitrogen. The nitrogen would freeze, forming a huge iceberg which would then float to the surface. Simple, and of course very fitting. An iceberg sent Titanic down, so an iceberg could bring her up!

All these crackpot plans ignored two important facts. Firstly, no one knew the exact spot where the Titanic had gone down. Secondly, everyone was assuming the ship was still in one piece. And that's where they were wrong.

So was it ever found?

Yes, the wreck of the Titanic was finally found, 73 years after the disaster. In 1985 a joint French-American expedition set out to try to find and photograph the wreck using the latest sonar technology. For five weeks the search went on in heavy seas, finding nothing. Then, early on the morning of 1st September, one of the underwater video cameras picked up a huge object. It was one of the sunken ship's giant boilers. Soon the cameras picked up more pictures of tangled steel and portholes. At last they had found the wreck of the Titanic.

The following year the team went back with Jason Junior – a robot armed with powerful cameras and lighting.

Amazingly, Jason Junior found the Titanic's crystal chandeliers, still intact, after 73 years at the bottom of the sea.

And what about the treasure?

The Titanic was in remarkable condition, but the ship had broken in two. The bow and stern (the back of the ship) lay 2,000 feet (650 metres) apart. In 1998 a large chunk of the ship's hull was raised using bags filled with diesel oil to float it to the surface. But the dream of raising the Titanic itself had to be abandoned - the sea wouldn't give it up.

Still, if the ship couldn't come to them, explorers could go to the ship. Since 1987, over 5,000 objects have been brought up from the Titanic and put on display around the world. Through these, we can get a fascinating snapshot of life on the most famous ship of all time.

Each item has its own history. A gold pocket watch recovered in 1987 belonged to Thomas Brown, who was travelling to America with his wife and 16-year-old daughter, Edith.

The pocket watch was restored to Edith when she was ninety-one, 75 years after she'd last seen it.

Other small treasures rescued from the deep include a bronze cherub from one of the staircases, coal from the engine room, a Chinese good luck pin, a corked bottle of olives, a bottle of champagne, a china potty, first class dinner plates, a bundle of toothpicks and a steward's cotton jacket marked with the name "Broome". Maybe it wasn't the gold and diamonds people had dreamed of, but it was still treasure of a kind.

So that's the end of the story?

Well, today people are just as fascinated as ever by the tragedy. Film director James Cameron had always been interested in the Titanic and decided to make a film to introduce the story to a new generation. Cameron started out with a budget of a mind-blowing $100 million. But that proved to be chicken feed. By the time he'd completed the picture he'd spent twice that amount. Critics predicted that Titanic would be the most expensive turkey ever made. But Cameron had the last laugh when the film was released in 1997. Titanic became the biggest box office success of all time and picked up a record 11 Oscars along the way!

Meanwhile, the Titanic remains at the bottom of the ocean. Somehow that only adds to its mystery. No other ship in history has captured the imagination of people all around the world in quite the same way. No other disaster has commanded so much attention for a whole century. The Titanic story is one of the great events of modern times. It happened during a Golden Age when people believed there was no limit to progress and invention. And the Titanic itself was the biggest boast of the age. It was longer, bigger, more powerful, more luxurious than any other ship ever built. That's why the sinking of the Titanic sent shock waves throughout the whole western world.

The Titanic was a man-made wonder. Yet on that terrible night of 14th April, 1912, the sea proved that no ship is "unsinkable".